my itty-bitty bio

Travis Kelce

Published in the United States of America by Cherry Lake Publishing
Ann Arbor, Michigan
www.cherrylakepublishing.com

Reading Adviser: Beth Walker Gambro, MS, Ed., Reading Consultant, Yorkville, IL
Illustrator: Leo Trinidad

Photo Credits: © Gary Hider/Dreamstime.com, 5; © Kim Reinick/Shutterstock, 7; © Zuma Press, Inc./Alamy Stock Photo, 9; © Sipa USA/Alamy Stock Photo, 11, 22; © UPI/Alamy Stock Photo, 13; © UPI/Alamy Stock Photo, 15; © dpa picture alliance/Alamy Stock Photo, 17; © AP Photo/Ashley Landis/ASSOCIATED PRESS, 19, 23; © G. Newman Lowrance via AP/ASSOCIATED PRESS, 21

Copyright © 2026 by Cherry Lake Publishing
All rights reserved. No part of this book may be reproduced or utilized in any form or by any means without written permission from the publisher.

Cherry Lake Press is an imprint of Cherry Lake Publishing Group

Library of Congress Cataloging-in-Publication Data has been filed and is available at catalog.loc.gov.

Printed in the United States of America

table of contents

My Story 4

Timeline 22

Glossary 24

Index 24

About the author: When not writing, Dr. Virginia Loh-Hagan serves as the Executive Director for AANAPISI Affairs and the APIDA Center at San Diego State University. She is also the Co-Executive Director of The Asian American Education Project. She lives in San Diego with her very tall husband and very naughty dogs.

About the illustrator: Leo Trinidad is a *New York Times* bestselling comic book artist, illustrator, and animator from Costa Rica. For more than 12 years, he's been creating content for children's books and TV shows. Leo created the first animated series ever produced in Central America and founded Rocket Cartoons, one of the most successful animation studios in Latin America. He is also the 2018 winner of the Central American Graphic Novel contest.

my story

I was born in 1989.

I am from Ohio.

I was a sports star in high school. I played football.

I played basketball.

I played baseball.

What sports do you like to play?

I played college football.

I was a **quarterback** and **tight end**.

I play **professional** football.

I played in many championship games.

I broke many records.

I'm one of the best tight ends of all time.

I love my brother. His name is Jason. He also played professional football.

He inspired me.

Who inspires you?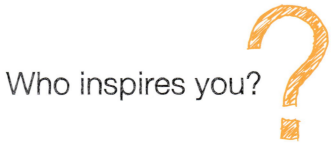

I have many fans. I have a business. I'm on TV. I have a **podcast**.

I support the community.

I'm a big fan of Taylor Swift.

I'm the biggest "**Swiftie**."

My legacy lives on. I work hard. I play hard.

I'm a role model.

What would you like to ask me?

timeline

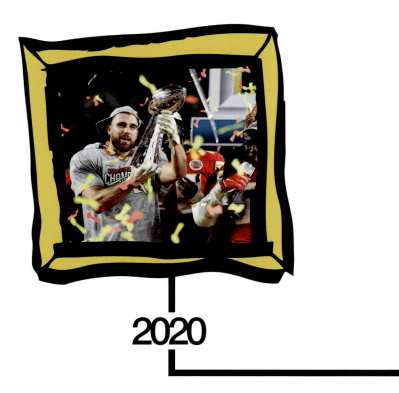

2020

1970

Born
1989

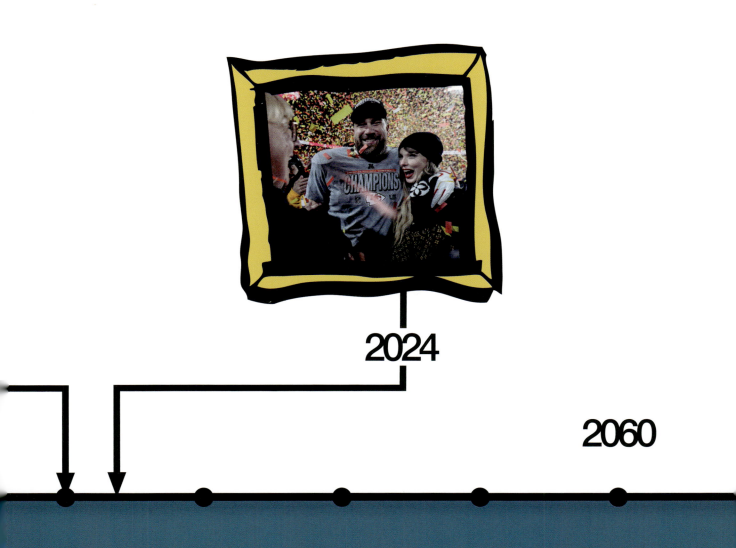

2024

2060

glossary

podcast (PAHD-kast) audio or video program with episodes about a specific topic

professional (pruh-FESH-nuhl) related to a job; describing when someone is paid for their work

quarterback (KWOHR-tuhr-bak) player who leads the offense and is responsible for calling plays and directing the team

Swiftie (SWIFT-ee) a member of Taylor Swift's fandom

tight end (TIEYT END) player who blocks on running plays or becomes a receiver on passing plays

index

birth, 4, 22

college, 8–9

family, 14–15
fans, 16–19
football, 6–21

Kansas City Chiefs (team), 11,13,15, 17, 19, 21–23
Kelce, Jason, 14–15

professional career, 10–21

Swift, Taylor, 18–19

talent, 6, 8, 12, 16, 20
timeline, 22–23